Passion

ALSO BY JUNE JORDAN

Passion

New Poems, 1977–1980

June Jordan
with a preface by the poet

Beacon Press ▪ Boston

Selections in this book have been previously published in *Nimrod,*
The New York Times, The Little Magazine, Essence, Callaloo, The Black
Collegian, and *Woman Poet.*

Grateful acknowledgment is made to Grove Press for permission to
quote from "The Heights of Macchu Picchu: IV," "The Dictators,"
and "The Woes and the Furies" that appeared in *Selected Poems of*
Pablo Neruda, translated by Ben Belitt. Copyright © 1961. Reprinted
by permission.

Beacon Press books are published under the auspices
of the Unitarian Universalist Association
Published simultaneously in Canada by
Fitzhenry & Whiteside Limited, Toronto

(hardcover)   9   8   7   6   5   4   3   2   1
(paperback)   9   8   7   6   5   4   3   2   1

Library of Congress Cataloging in Publication Data

Jordan, June, 1936-
    Passion, new poems, 1977–1980.

    I. Title.
PS3560.073P3   1980   811'.54   80–66073
ISBN 0–8070–3218–2
ISBN 0–8070–3219–0 (pbk.)

Dedicated to
Everybody scared as I used to be

Contents

For the Sake of a People's Poetry: Walt Whitman and the Rest of Us

In America, the father is white: It is he who inaugurated the experiment of this republic. It is he who sailed his way into slave ownership. It is he who availed himself of my mother: the African woman whose function was miserably defined by his desirings, or his rage. It is he who continues to dominate the destiny of the Mississippi River, the Blue Ridge Mountains, and the life of my son. Understandably, then, I am curious about this man.

Most of the time my interest can be characterized as wary, at best. Other times, it is the interest a pedestrian feels for the fast-traveling truck about to smash into him. Or her. Again. And at other times it is the curiosity of a stranger trying to figure out the system of the language that excludes her name and all of the names of all of her people. It is this last that leads me to the poet Walt Whitman.

Trying to understand the system responsible for every boring, inaccessible, irrelevant, derivative, and pretentious poem that is glued to the marrow of required readings in American classrooms, or trying to understand the system responsible for the exclusion of every hilarious, amazing, visionary, pertinent, and unforgettable poet from N.E.A. grants and from national publications, I come back to Walt Whitman.

What in the hell happened to him? Wasn't he a white man? Wasn't he some kind of a father to American literature? Didn't he talk about this New World? Didn't he see it? Didn't he sing this New World, this

America, on a New World, an American scale of his own visionary invention?

It so happens that Walt Whitman is the one white father who shares the systematic disadvantages of his heterogeneous offspring trapped inside a closet that is, in reality, as huge as the continental spread of North and South America. What Whitman envisioned we, the people and the poets of the New World, embody. He has been punished for the political meaning of his vision. We are being punished for the moral questions that our very lives provoke.

At home as a child I learned the poetry of the Bible and the poetry of Paul Laurence Dunbar. As a student, I diligently followed orthodox directions from *The Canterbury Tales* right through *The Waste Land* by that consummate Anglophile whose name I can never remember. And I kept waiting. It was, I thought, all right to deal with daffodils in the seventeenth century on an island as much like Manhattan as I resemble Queen Mary. But what about Dunbar? When was he coming up again? And where were the Black poets altogether? And who were the women poets I might reasonably emulate? And wasn't there, ever, a great poet who was crazy about Brooklyn or furious about war? And I kept waiting. And I kept writing my own poetry. And I kept reading apparently underground poetry: poetry kept strictly off campus. And I kept reading the poetry of so many gifted students when I became a teacher myself, and I kept listening to the wonderful poetry of the multiplying numbers of my friends who were and who are New

World poets until I knew, for a fact, that there was and that there is an American, a New World, poetry that is as personal, as public, as irresistible, as quick, as necessary, as unprecedented, as representative, as exalted, as speakably commonplace, and as musical, as an emergency phone call.

But I didn't know about Walt Whitman. Yes: I had heard about this bohemian, this homosexual even, who wrote something about The Captain and The Lilacs, but nobody ever told me he was crucial to a native American literature. Not only was Whitman not required reading, in the sense that Wordsworth and Robert Herrick are required reading, he was, on the contrary, presented as a rather hairy buffoon suffering from a childish proclivity for exercise and open air. Nevertheless, it is through the study of all the poems and all the ideas of this particular white father that I have reached a tactical, if not strategic, understanding of the racist, sexist, and anti-American predicament that condemns most New World writing to peripheral/small press/unpublished manuscript status.

Before these United States, the great poems of the world earned their luster through undeniable forms of spontaneous popularity: Generations of a people chose to memorize and then to further elaborate and then to impart these songs to the next generation. I am talking about people: African families and Greek families and the families of the Hebrew tribes and all that multitude to whom the Bhagavad-Gita is as daily as the sun. If these poems were not always religious, they were certainly moral in motive, or in accomplishment, or both. None of these great poems could be mistaken for the poetry of another country, another time; you do not find a single helicopter taking off or landing in any of the sonnets of Elizabethan England, nor do you run across Jamaican rice and peas in any of the psalms. Evidently, one criterion for great poetry used to be the requirements of cultural nationalism.

But with the advent of the 36-year-old poet Walt Whitman, the phenomenon of a people's poetry, or great poetry and its spontaneous popularity, could no longer be assumed. The physical immensity and the far-flung population of this New World decisively separated the poet from the suitable means to produce and to distribute his poetry. Now there would have to be intermediaries—critics and publishers— whose marketplace principles of scarcity would, logically, oppose them to populist traditions of art. In place of the democratic concepts, elitist Old World concepts would, logically, govern their policies; in the context of such considerations, an American literary establishment antithetical to the New World meanings of America took root. And this is one reason why the pre-eminently American white father of American poetry is practically unknown outside the realm of caricature and rumor in his own country.

As a matter of fact, if you hope to hear about Whitman, your best bet is to leave home: Ignore prevailing American criticism and, instead, ask anybody anywhere else in the world this question: As

Shakespeare is to England, Dante to Italy, Tolstoi to Russia, Goethe to Germany, Agostinho Neto to Angola, Pablo Neruda to Chile, Mao Tse-tung to China, and Ho Chi Minh to Vietnam, who is the great American writer, the distinctively American poet, the giant American "literatus"? Undoubtedly, the answer will be *Walt Whitman*. He is the poet who wrote:

A man's body at auction,
(For before the war I often go to the slave-mart and watch the sale,)
I help the auctioneer, the sloven does not half know his business.

Gentlemen look on this wonder,
Whatever the bids of the bidders they cannot be high enough for it

"I Sing the Body Electric"

I ask you today: Who in America would publish those lines? They are all wrong! In the first place, there is nothing obscure, nothing contrived, nothing an ordinary straphanger in the subway would be puzzled by. In the second place, the voice of those lines is intimate and direct at once: It is the voice of the poet who assumes that he speaks to an equal and that he need not fear that equality; on the contrary, the intimate distance between the poet and the reader is a distance that assumes there is everything important, between them, to be shared. And what is poetic about a line of words that runs as long as a regular, a spoken idea? You could more easily imagine an actual human being speaking such lines than you could imagine an artist composing them in a room carefully separated from other rooms of a house, carefully separated from other lives of a family: This can't be poetry. Besides, these lines apparently serve an expressly moral purpose! Then is this didactic/political writing? This cannot be good poetry. And, in fact, you will never see, for example, *The New Yorker* publishing a poem marked by such splendid deficiencies.

Consider the inevitable, the irresistible simplicity of that enormous moral idea:

Gentlemen look on this wonder,
Whatever the bids of the bidders they cannot be high enough for it . . .
This is not only one man, this the father of those who shall be
fathers in their turns,
In him the start of populous states and rich republics,
Of him countless immortal lives with countless embodiments and
enjoyments.

"I Sing the Body Electric"

This is not an idea generally broadcast in America. It is an idea to violate the marketplace: The poet is trying to rescue a human being while even the poem cannot be saved from the insolence of marketplace evaluation!

Indeed Walt Whitman and the traceable descendants of Whitman, those who follow his democratic faith into obviously New World forms of experience and art, they suffer from the same establishment rejection and contempt that forced this archetypal American genius to publish, distribute, and review his own work—by himself. The descendants I have in mind include those unmistakably contemporaneous young poets who base themselves upon domesticities such as disco, Las Vegas, McDonald's, and forty-dollar running shoes. Also within the Whitman tradition, Black and Third World poets traceably transform, and further, the egalitarian sensibility that isolates that one white father from his more powerful compatriots. And I am thinking of those feminist poets who are evidently intent upon speaking with a maximal number and diversity of other American lives. And I am thinking of such first-rank heroes of the New World as Pablo Neruda and Agostinho Neto. Except for these last two, New World poets are overwhelmingly forced to publish their own works, or seek the commitment of a small press or else give it up entirely. That is to say, the only peoples who can test or verify the meaning of America as a democratic state, as a pluralistic culture, are the very peoples whose contribution to a national vision and discovery meet with general ridicule and disregard. A democratic state does not, after all, exist for the few, but for the many. A democratic state is not proven by the welfare of the strong but by the welfare of the weak. And unless that many, that manifold constitution of diverse peoples can be seen as integral to the national art/the national consciousness, you might as well mean only Czechoslovakia when you talk about the U.S.A., or only Ireland, or merely France, or exclusively white men.

The fate of Pablo Neruda differs from the other Whitman descendants because Neruda was born into a sovereign New World country where a majority of the citizens did not mistake themselves for Englishmen or long to find themselves struggling, at most, with cucumber sandwiches and tea. He was never European. His anguish was not aroused by three-piece suits and rolled umbrellas. When he cries, toward the conclusion of *The Heights of Macchu Picchu*, "Arise to birth with me, my brother," he plainly does not allude to Lord or Colonel Anybody At All. As he writes, earlier, in that amazing poem:

I came by another way, river by river, street after street,
city by city, one bed and another,
forcing the salt of my mask through a wilderness;
and there, in the shame of the ultimate hovels, lampless and fireless,
lacking bread or a stone or a stillness, alone in myself,
I whirled at my will, dying the death that was mine.

Of course Neruda has not escaped all of the untoward consequences common to Whitman descendants. American critics and translators never weary of asserting that Neruda is a quote great unquote poet despite the political commitment of his art and despite the artistic consequences of that commitment. Specifically, Neruda's self-conscious decision to write in a manner readily comprehensible to the masses of his countrymen and his self-conscious decision to specify outright the United Fruit Company when that was the instigating subject of his poem become unfortunate moments in an otherwise supposedly sublime, not to mention surrealist, deeply Old World and European but nonetheless Chilean case history. To assure the validity of this perspective, the usual American critic and translator presents you with a smattering of the unfortunate, ostensibly political poetry and, on the other hand, buries you under volumes of Neruda's early work that antedates the Spanish Civil War or, in other words, that antedates Neruda's serious conversion to a political world view.

This kind of artistically indefensible censorship would have you perceive chasmic and even irreconcilable qualitative differences between the poet who wrote:

You, my antagonist, in that splintering dream
like the bristling glass of gardens, like a menace
of ruinous bells, volleys
of blackening ivy at the perfume's center
enemy of the great hipbones my skin has touched
with a harrowing dew

"The Woes and the Furies"

and the poet who wrote, some twenty years later,
these lines from the poem entitled "The Dictators":

lament was perpetual and fell, like a plant and its pollen,
forcing a lightless increase in the blinded, big leaves.
And bludgeon by bludgeon, on the terrible waters,
scale over scale in the bog,
the snout filled with silence and slime
and vendetta was born.

According to prevalent American criticism, that later
poem by Neruda represents a lesser achievement pre-
cisely because it can be understood by more people,
more easily, than the first. It is also denigrated be-
cause it attacks a keystone of the Old World, namely
dictatorship, or, in other words, power and privilege
for the few.

The peculiar North American vendetta against
Walt Whitman, against the first son of this democratic
union, should be further fathomed: Neruda's emi-
nence is now acknowledged on international levels;
his work profoundly affects many North American
poets who do not realize, because they have never
been shown, the North American/the Walt Whitman
origins for so much that is singular and worthy in the
poetry of Neruda. You will even find American critics
who congratulate Neruda for overcoming the "Whit-
manese" content of his art! This perfidious arrogance
is as calculated as it is common. You cannot persuade
anyone seriously familiar with Neruda's life and art

that he could have found cause, at any point, to disagree with the tenets, the analysis, and the authentic New World vision presented by Walt Whitman in his essay "Democratic Vistas," which remains the most signal and persuasive manifesto of New World thinking and belief in print.

Let me define my terms in brief: New World does not mean New England. New World means non-European; it means new, it means big, it means heterogeneous, it means unknown, it means free, it means an end to feudalism, caste, privilege, and the violence of power. It means *wild* in the sense that a tree growing away from the earth enacts a wild event. It means *democratic* in the sense that, as Whitman wrote:

I believe a leaf of grass is no less than the journey-work of the stars . . .
And a mouse is miracle enough to stagger sextillions of infidels.

"Song of Myself"

New World means, in Whitman's words, "I keep as delicate around the bowels as around the head and heart." New World means, again, to quote Whitman, "By God! I will accept nothing which all cannot have their counterpart of on the same terms." In "Democratic Vistas," Whitman declared,

As the greatest lessons of Nature through the universe are perhaps the lessons of variety and freedom, the same present the greatest lessons also

in New World politics and progress . . .
Sole among nationalities, these States have
assumed the task to put in forms of history, power
and practicality, on areas of amplitude rivaling the
operations of the physical kosmos, the moral
political speculations of ages, long, long deferr'd,
the democratic republican principle, and the theory
of development and perfection by voluntary
standards, and self-reliance.

Listen to this white man; he is so weird! Here he is
calling aloud for an American, a democratic spirit, an
American, a democratic idea that could morally con-
strain and coordinate the material body of U.S.A.
affluence and piratical outreach, more than a hun-
dred years ago. He wrote:

The great poems, Shakespeare included, are
poisonous to the idea of the pride and dignity of
the common people, the lifeblood of democracy.
The models of our literature, as we get it from
other lands, ultra marine, have had their birth in
courts, and bask'd and grown in castle sunshine; all
smells of princes' favors . . . Do you call those
genteel little creatures American poets? Do you
term that perpetual, pistareen, paste-pot work,
American art, American drama, taste, verse? . . .
We see the sons and daughters of The New World,
ignorant of its genius, not yet inaugurating the
native, the universal, and the near, still importing
the distant, the partial, the dead.

Abhorring the "thin sentiment of parlors, parasols, piano-song, tinkling rhymes," Whitman conjured up a poetry of America, a poetry of democracy that would not "mean the smooth walks, trimm'd hedges, poseys and nightingales of the English poets, but the whole orb, with its geologic history, the Kosmos, carrying fire and snow that rolls through the illimitable areas, light as a feather, though weighing billions of tons."

Well, what happened?

Whitman went ahead and wrote the poetry demanded by his vision. He became, by thousands upon thousands of words, a great American poet:

There was a child went forth every day,
And the first object he look'd upon, that object he became,
And that object became part of him for the day or a certain part
of the day,
Or for many years or stretching cycles of years.

The early lilacs became part of this child,
And grass and white and red morning-glories, and white and red
clover, and the song of the phoebe-bird,

"There Was a Child Went Forth"

And elsewhere he wrote:

It avails not, time nor place—distance avails not,
I am with you, you men and women of a generation, or ever so
many generations hence,
Just as you feel when you look on the river and sky, so I felt,
Just as any of you is one of a living crowd, I was one of a crowd,
Just as you are refresh'd by the gladness of the river and the bright
flow, I was refresh'd,
Just as you stand and lean
on the rail, yet hurry with the swift
current, I stood yet was hurried,
Just as you look on the numberless masts of ships and the thick-
stemm'd pipes of steamboats,
I look'd . . .

"Crossing Brooklyn Ferry"

This great American poet of democracy as cosmos,
this poet of a continent as consciousness, this poet of
the many people as one people, this poet of a diction
comprehensible to all, of a vision insisting on each, of
a rhythm/a rhetorical momentum to transport the
reader from the Brooklyn ferry into the hills of Alabama
and back again, of line after line of bodily, con-
crete detail that constitutes the mysterious, the cellu-
lar tissues of a nation indivisible but dependent upon
and astonishing in its diversity, this white father of a
great poetry deprived of its spontaneous popularity/a
great poetry hidden away from the ordinary people it
celebrates so well, he has been, again and again, cast

aside as an undisciplined poseur, a merely freak eruption of prolix perversities.

Last year, the *New York Times Book Review* saw fit to import a European self-appointed critic of American literature to address the question: Is there a great American poet? Since this visitor was ignorant of the philosophy and the achievements of Walt Whitman, the visitor, Denis Donoghue, comfortably excluded every possible descendant of Whitman from his erstwhile cerebrations: Only one woman was mentioned. (She, needless to add, did not qualify.) No poets under fifty, and not one Black or Third World poet, received even cursory assessment. Not one poet of distinctively New World values, and their formal embodiment, managed to dent the illiterate suavity of Donoghue's public display.

This *New York Times* event perpetuates American habits of beggarly, absurd deference to the Old World. And these habits bespeak more than marketplace intrusions into cultural realms: We erase ourselves through self-hatred, we lend our silence to the American anti-American process whereby anything and anyone special to this nation state becomes liable to condemnation because it is what it is, truly.

Against self-hatred there is Whitman and there are all of the New World poets who insistently devise legitimate varieties of cultural nationalism. There is Whitman and all of the poets whose lives have been baptized by witness to blood, by witness to cataclysmic, political confrontations from the Civil War through the Civil Rights Era, through the Women's

Movement, and on and on through the conflicts between the hungry and the fat, the wasteful, the bullies.

In the poetry of The New World, you meet with a reverence for the material world that begins with a reverence for human life, an intellectual trust in sensuality as a means of knowledge and of unity, an easily deciphered system of reference, aspiration to a believable, collective voice and, consequently, emphatic preference for broadly accessible language and/or "spoken" use of language, a structure of forward energies that interconnects apparently discrete or even conflictual elements, saturation by quotidian data, and a deliberate balancing of perception with vision: a balancing of sensory report with moral exhortation.

All of the traceable descendants of Whitman have met with an establishment, an academic, reception disgracefully identical: Except for the New World poets who live and write beyond the boundaries of the U.S.A., the offspring of this one white father encounter everlasting marketplace disparagement as crude or optional or simplistic or, as Whitman himself wrote, "hankering, gross, mystical, nude."

I too am a descendant of Walt Whitman. And I am not by myself struggling to tell the truth about this history of so much land and so much blood, of so much that should be sacred and so much that has been desecrated and annihilated boastfully.

My brothers and my sisters of this New World, we remember that, as Whitman said,

I do not trouble my spirit to vindicate itself or be understood,
I see that the elementary laws never apologize.

"Song of Myself"

We do not apologize because we are not Emily Dick-
inson, Ezra Pound, T. S. Eliot, Wallace Stevens,
Robert Lowell, or Elizabeth Bishop. If we are nothing
to them, to those who love them, they are nothing to
us! Or, as Whitman exclaimed: "I exist as I am, that is
enough."

New World poetry moves into and beyond the
light of the lives of Walt Whitman, Pablo Neruda,
Agostinho Neto, Gabriela Mistral, Langston Hughes,
Margaret Walker, and Edward Brathwaite.

I follow this movement with my own life. I am calm
and I am smiling as we go. Is it not written some-
where very near to me:

A man's body at auction . . .
Gentlemen, look on this wonder,
Whatever the bids of the bidders they cannot be high enough for it

And didn't that weird white father predict this truth
that is always growing:

I swear to you the architects shall appear without fail,
I swear to you they will understand you and justify you,
The greatest among them shall be he who best knows you, and
encloses all and is faithful to all,

He and the rest shall not forget you, they shall perceive that you
are not an iota less than they,
You shall be fully glorified in them.

"A Song of the Rolling Earth"

Walt Whitman and all of the New World poets com-
ing after him, we, too, go on singing this America.

JUNE JORDAN
NEW YORK CITY 1979

Poem for Nana

What will we do
when there is nobody left
to kill?

■

40,000 gallons of oil gushing into
the ocean
But I
sit on top this mountainside above
the Pacific
checking out the flowers
the California poppies orange
as I meet myself in heat
                    I'm wondering
where's the Indians?

                        all this filmstrip territory
                        all this cowboy sagaland:
                        not
                        a single Indian
                        in sight

40,000 gallons gushing up poison
from the deepest seabeds
every hour

40,000 gallons
while
experts international
while
new pollutants
swallow the unfathomable
still:

   no Indians

I'm staring hard around me
past the pinks the poppies and the precipice
that let me see the wide Pacific
unsuspecting
even trivial
by virtue of its vast surrender

I am a woman searching for her savagery
even if it's doomed

Where are the Indians?

■

Crow Nose
Little Bear
Slim Girl
Black Elk
Fox Belly

the people of the sacred trees
and rivers precious to the stars that told
old stories to the night

how do we follow after you?

falling
snow before the firelight
and buffalo as brothers
to the man

how do we follow into that?

■

They found her facedown
where she would be dancing
to the shadow drums that humble
birds to silent
        flight

They found her body held
its life dispelled
by ice
my life burns to destroy

Anna Mae Pictou Aquash
slain on The Trail of Broken Treaties
bullet lodged in her brain/hands
and fingertips
dismembered

who won the only peace
that cannot pass
from mouth to mouth

■

Memory should agitate
the pierced bone crack
of one in pushed-back horror
pushed-back pain
as when I call out looking for my face
among the wounded coins
to toss about
or out
entirely
the legends of Geronimo
of Pocahontas
now become a squat
pedestrian cement inside the tomb
of all my trust

as when I feel you isolate
among the hungers of the trees
a trembling
hidden tinder so long unsolicited
by flame

as when I accept my sister dead
when there should be
a fluid holiness
of spirits wrapped around the world
redeemed by women
whispering communion

■

I find my way by following your spine

Your heart indivisible from my real wish
we
compelled the moon into the evening when
you said, "No,
I will not let go
of your hand."

■

Now I am diving for a tide to take me everywhere

Below
the soft Pacific spoils
a purple girdling of the globe
impregnable

■

Last year the South African Minister of Justice
described Anti-Government Disturbances as
Part of a Worldwide Trend toward the
Breakdown of Established Political and Cultural
Orders

■

God knows I hope he's right.

Poem for the Poet Alexis DeVeaux

The shadows of the body
blue and not blue
brown and not blue
blue and not brown
intimate
insist

deify
the thing within
all of it
within the body shadows
from the rose

herself

Current Events

He did not!
He did so!
He did not!
I'm telling you!
You lie!
Uh-unhh.
You're kidding me!
Cross my heart and hope to die!
Really?
No shit!
Yeah?
Yeah!
The What?
The Ayatollah Khomeini!
Getoutahere.
Square business!
The Who?
The Ayatollah Khomeini of Iran!
So?
So he said it!
Big deal.
That's what I'm saying:
Thursday
November 15th
1979
the headline reads:
IRAN SET TO
FREE WOMEN
AND BLACKS
Run that by, again!

Okay:
Thursday
November 15th
No! Not that part!
Just wait a second:
Thursday
November 15th
1979 and
this is the headline:
IRAN SET TO
FREE WOMEN
AND BLACKS:
See now
I told you it's a big deal!
How was I supposed to know?
Girl
you better keep up with the news!
Yeah, yeah:
I'm planning to!

Poem about The Head of a Negro
Painted by Peter Paul Rubens, 1577–1640

Up the shaken stairway
Back four hundred years
Before the meaningless emancipation
In an arbitrary corner
Of an old room
I find the face a tender contradiction
To the not entirely invisible bullet
Hole
The circling blush macabre as its history
Told into the left temple of the humbling skull

I find a man
the mother of mysterious crime
I find a man
the mother of me

The sweet the burden of the air around the head
that must look down
down
down into the flesh
down
down
down into the muscle of the flesh
down
down
down into the bleeding of the muscle
down
down
down into the candle of the blood

The Morning on the Mountains

The morning on the mountains where the mist
diffuses
down into the depths of the leaves
of the ash and oak trees
trickling toward the complexion of the whole lake
cold
even though the overlooking sky
so solemnly vermilion
sub-divides/the
seething stripes as soft
as sweet as the opening
of your mouth

"The Rationale" or "She Drove Me Crazy"

"Well, your Honor,
it was late. Three A.M. Nobody on the streets.
And I was movin along, mindin my business when
suddenly there she was
alone
by herself
gleamin under the street lamp. I thought
'Whoa. Check this out? Hey, Baby! What's
happenin?,' I said under my breath.
And I tried to walk past but she was lookin
so good and
the gleam and the shine and
the beautiful lines of her
body sittin out there
alone
by herself
made me wild. I went wild. But
I looked all around to see where her
owner/where the man in her life could
probably be. But no show. She was out.
By herself. On the street:
As fine, as ready to go as anythin you could
ever possibly want to see so
I checked out myself: what's this?
Then I lost my control; I couldn't resist.
What did she expect? She looked foreign
besides and small and sexy
and fast
by the curb. So I lost my control and

I forced her open and I entered
her body and I poured myself
into her
pumpin for all I was worth
wild as I was
when you caught me

third time apprehended
for the theft of a Porsche."

Case in Point

A friend of mine who raised six daughters and
who never wrote what she regards as serious
until she
was fifty-three
tells me there is no silence peculiar
to the female

I have decided I have something to say
about female silence: so to speak
these are my 2¢ on the subject:
2 weeks ago I was raped for the second
time in my life the first occasion
being a whiteman and the most recent
situation being a blackman actually
head of the local NAACP

Today is 2 weeks after the fact
of that man straddling
his knees either side of my chest
his hairy arm and powerful left hand
forcing my arms and my hands over my head
flat to the pillow while he rammed
what he described as his quote big dick
unquote into my mouth
and shouted out: "D'ya want to swallow
my big dick; well, do ya?"

He was being rhetorical.
My silence was peculiar
to the female.

Poem of Personal Greeting for Fidel,
on the occasion of his trip to the United Nations, October 1979

When I thought about you hiding away up
in the hills below Miami it was
frequently/before and after errands
to the drugstore or a toddling promenade
to show my three-year-old the ways
of a river (filthy but nonetheless) headed south
where I pictured you hilarious
and stalwart
in a Robin Hood Bodega

Any regular Goliath
could pull apart that arsenal (I thought)
of leaves
sleeping bags
mosquitoes
individual canteen supplies of muddy water
scalding chocolate in tin cups
around the Girl Scout fires

But you arrived
inside the stadium
inside the multitudinous *caminos/avenidas*
de la libertad
filled by half a million hot compadres
like a tidal waving
over the formerly inert
dirt of the lovely
island

To amend the broken knees the incredulities
of Harlem/of myself apostate to all miracles
before you
you came looming indisputable
a very hirsute
Spanish-speaking hero
forcibly translated to the English *what*
goes around comes around: what comes through
Cuba goes around the world

20 years additional and now
my son (a man to whom I mail the clippings
from your visit to New York) walks quietly
high but invisible among the sandhills of Nebraska
thinking rather well of Sandinista possibilities
for patience and for
victory and
plotting to return by rail and route he must lay
down himself
against the isolating miles of flat America
and nonetheless now
el norteamericano media
disgrace the meaning the persevering heroics
of your moral pace among the humble
urgencies that scab the whole incorporated
planet/the media
dismiss the grace of your arithmetic
transliterating bullets into butter
hospitals and books for children
and

this is to let you know that nonetheless
that now
I will drink new wine
tilt the bottle toward Nebraska
lift a glass toward your bearded image on the screen
and I will say *bienvenido*
y salud
because *what*
goes around comes around: what comes through
Cuba goes around the world!

Newport Jazz Festival:
Saratoga Springs and Especially
about George Benson and everyone who
was listening

We got to the point of balloons all of us
held aloft/a tender tapping at the skin
of coloring translucent
and
nothing was too deep but the incendiary/slow the rainy/
rainbow crowded surface did not keep
anybody from caring enough to undertake a random
openhanded sharing of much hefty
toke equipment/smoke
was passing by like kisses in the air
where little girls
blew bubbles
benedictory below the softly bloated
clouds

While the trumpets lifted sterling
curvilinear tonalities
to turn the leaves down low/well-
lit by glowing globes of candlelight
that man was singing

That man was singing
Baby
Baby if you come with me
I'll make you my own Dairy Queen
or if that's locked we'll find an all-night Jack-
in-the-Box steak sandwich/fried onion rings
blackcherry/strawberry/butterscotch/shake
blackcherry/strawberry/butterscotch
shake
blackcherry/strawberry/butterscotch
shake

Baby
if you come now Baby if you if you Baby if you come
now

Patricia's Poem

"Listen
after I have set the table
folded the scottowel into napkins
cooked this delicious eggplant stuffed
with bulghur wheat
then baked the whole thing under a careful
covering of mozzarella cheese
and
said my grace

don't you bring Anita Bryant/Richard
Pryor/the Justices of the Supreme Court/don't
you bring any of those people in here
to spoil my digestive processes
and ruin
my dinner

you hear?"

"hey, Baby: You married?"

Willie at The Golden Grill
came straight from work to drink tequila
and explain this to me at eleven
P.M.
around the corner of the jukebox
where we partially ignore
the music

planning "to
break into business here
in Saratoga
at the racetrack or
whatever"

at 25
he's got 5 years before a marriage
hits him although
it could happen to you sooner
than you plan or so he solemnly
agrees

We do a slowdrool dance
him thin underneath the regulation blue
baseball cap
peaked carefully above the pretty eyes
and not much taller than I am

"I didn't have time to change my clothes"
Willie tells me/smiling true
to the rhythm of the melody of his mouth
is thick

"Around here?" he continues: "The disco is
THE RAFTERS: The best lightshow the best
DeeJay in New York State! And
I'm the bouncer!"

I watch the directions Willie gives me
carrying his fingers casual across
the jukebox title cards
lit from below

"Come up to THE RAFTERS
any Wednesday/Friday/Saturday night"
he says
"And"
he emphasizes quietly
"It'll be on me!"

"Yeah?" I ask him.

"Yeah!" he answers me:
"Why not?!"

TV Is Easy Next to Life

Check out Sidney Poitier as Noble Savage
and there's Rock Hudson playing Bwana
see him shoot down Noble Savage/Former
Childhood Playmate in the Jungle/shoot his
wife and all the tribe be decimated
by All A Big Mistake co-starring
U.S. Army rifles and Colonial Lust
then Bwana chase him playmate/Sidney:
"Noble Savage and your baby son, don't run!"
Sidney halts. The cameras zoom to large
native eyes of the African man who cries out:
"No! You kill my wife you kill my people:
No more talking!" But
Rock is like a rock: "Don't be a fool!" he
shouts back: "That was a mistake. Let
me explain!"
Cut to this advertisement:
"Now! Before Africa goes up in flames—
You can own these magnificent gems that
are everyone's best friend these days
at only $8.95 a half carat
yes
genuine
natural diamonds

The world's diamond deposits will
soon be exhausted. With diamonds
increasing in value 4 times in 15 years
it seems reasonable to suppose the value
of these diamonds will rise even more sharply when
South Africa explodes into full-scale war (comma)
which it could do momentarily (period) But regardless
if war comes (comma) this is a risk-free (comma) in
fact (comma) brilliant purchase (period)
Get several as gifts (period)
But hurry (period)"

TV is easy next to life
Check out the Noble Savage adamant against
the conversation the dialog the seminar the National
Commission to Investigate the slaughtering of his
wife and people
Sidney runs. But Bwana
quite determined to discuss these matters takes
a bead on Noble Savage fells him
to the forest floor from which my brother man
will rise no more
Another accident: Behold the childhood playmate of
the jungle dying now
he's dead
and Bwana says he'll raise the baby boy survivor
by himself instead
                    to be a what
                    for whom?
Ah, questions! Questions!

The woman who left the house this morning
more or less on her way to Mississippi more
or less through Virginia in order to pack and get back to
New York on her way to The People's Republic of
Angola
was
stopped in Washington D.C. by an undercover
agent for the C.I.A. offering to help her with
her bags

The woman who came to the house tonight with
her boy baby Ché on the way to Philly
for a showdown with Customs that wants to deport both
of them
to Venezuela because Ché's
father months ago ducked out
entirely
she
just offered to make me chickweed tea
for my runny nose cold

"You know what I have? A desk that's big enough," Sara
had said and which I could see now as we sat opposite
the bathtub in the kitchen of her newplace
where we talked away a good part of the afternoon re-
considering sex into a status satellite to dialog/work
hanging out/sport while another a third poet currently
doing what she does in Seattle came into the room
by cassette

"I have loved you assiduously" Trazana Beverly's voice
advertising *for colored girls* cracks me up on my
way to the airport/*assiduously* on the fm (yeah Zaki!) on
my way to pick up Louise wiped out by Cambridge where
she proved the muse is female on
paper
and
all this stuff going on and my lover wants to know
am I a feminist or what and what does the question
mean I mean
or *what*?

An Explanation Always Follows

Rose and ivory roses open among
us
at breakfast/the roses slope into the smoky
crystal of the silver-tipped vase

carved mahogany
chairs with weathered leather
seats
hold the sleepers upright

Slicing a small peach the older
man with steep
European accent
pops
a morsel of the peach into his mouth

savoring the fruit he
does not masticate the morsel
quite discreetly/I
must avert my eyes or
witness the entire process: tongue
teeth and peach enmeshed
degenerate

Now comes volunteer expatiation on allegedly
famous porn districts in Germany
(The Reeperbahn in Hamburg
Brewer's yeast and potency
yesterday's sperm count)

the older man
before cracking into soft-boiled eggs
(and balancing the knife in his right
hand with only four of the five
fingernails apparently
clean)
looks up to query my
increasing reticence

"Why," he questions me: "Don't you want to be seduced?!"

Letter to the Local Police

Dear Sirs:

I have been enjoying the law and order of our
community throughout the past three months since
my wife and I, our two cats, and miscellaneous
photographs of the six grandchildren belonging to
our previous neighbors (with whom we were very
close) arrived in Saratoga Springs which is clearly
prospering under your custody

Indeed, until yesterday afternoon and despite my
vigilant casting about, I have been unable to discover
a single instance of reasons for public-spirited concern,
much less complaint

You may easily appreciate, then, how it is that
I write to your office, at this date, with utmost
regret for the lamentable circumstances that force
my hand

Speaking directly to the issue of moment:

I have encountered a regular profusion of certain
unidentified roses, growing to no discernible purpose,
and according to no perceptible control, approximately
one quarter mile west of the Northway, on the southern
side

To be specific, there are practically thousands of
the aforementioned abiding in perpetual near riot
of wild behavior, indiscriminate coloring, and only
the Good Lord Himself can say what diverse soliciting
of promiscuous cross-fertilization

As I say, these roses, no matter what the apparent
background, training, tropistic tendencies, age,
or color, do not demonstrate the least inclination
toward categorization, specified allegiance, resolute
preference, consideration of the needs of others, nor
any other minimal traits of decency

May I point out that I did not assiduously seek out
this colony, as it were, and that these certain
unidentified roses remain open to viewing even by
children, with or without suitable supervision

(My wife asks me to append a note as regards the
seasonal but nevertheless seriously licentious
phenomenon of honeysuckle under the moon that one may
apprehend at the corner of Nelson and Main

However, I have recommended that she undertake direct
correspondence with you, as regards this: yet
another civic disturbance in our midst)

I am confident that you will devise and pursue
appropriate legal response to the roses in question
If I may aid your efforts in this respect, please
do not hesitate to call me into consultation

                              Respectfully yours,

Found Poem

Three stars: "Flaming Feather"
(1952)
A band of vigilantes rides
to the rescue of a white woman
captured by a tribe
of renegade Indians.

(1 hr. 30 min.)

Poem about a Night Out: Michael: Goodbye for a While

For Michael Harper

There had been death   There had been fire
and you would recommend Irish
whiskey saying "It's better than bourbon
smoother than scotch" and if I
replied, saying "Michael
the smoke tree sports the most infinitesimal
and linear blossomings
plus
perfectly elliptical leaves" you
might very well remark
"Uh-huh" and then inquire (the way
you did when you were pulling out the Volvo
and I ran over to the car alarmed at that)
"D'you need anything?" (gesturing to the stuff
in the backseat) "Rilke's
Duino Elegies, or anything?" the same
way you said (down to the local
disco after this guy about gave
it away to the beat that was not
that big) "Tell me
when you want me to kill him. And
I will."
There had been death   There had been fire
And the last night began behind the Fleetwood
Cadillac which the disco lady owner mo-
mentarily held beside the curbstone
boxes up on Broadway and you (laughing)
dropped my letters into LOCAL
while Barbara and Sonia and Robert
yelled, "Michael!"

then the saturnine the extremely pregnant
waitress told our table "If
you want anything, just wave"
while Peter rapped to me about Barbara
while Robert rapped to Barbara
about himself
while you never sat down
      you never sat down

the red rim of your ears
red throughout the whole earlier
dinnertime
red from the grieving/there had been
death there had been
fire
around the edges of your head
and here we were at five A.M. alive
alive
a silver lunacy flying small above a few
dark conifers but inside
the crowd of us was singing to the highway
well
you loved me
then you snubbed
me
now what can I do
I'm still in love with you
seeing the Japanese smoke among the mountains

then rolling into it
a u-turn on the highway
and the smoke among the mountains
and
didn't we sing
didn't we sing

Earth Angel
Earth Angel
Will you be mi-ine

and

didn't you never
never
sit down!

Poem about Police Violence

Tell me something
what you think would happen if
everytime they kill a black boy
then we kill a cop
everytime they kill a black man
then we kill a cop

you think the accident rate would lower
subsequently?

sometimes the feeling like amaze me baby
comes back to my mouth and I am quiet
like Olympian pools from the running the
mountainous snows under the sun

sometimes thinking about the 12th House of the Cosmos
or the way your ear ensnares the tip
of my tongue or signs that I have never seen
like DANGER WOMEN WORKING

I lose consciousness of ugly bestial rabid
and repetitive affront as when they tell me
18 cops in order to subdue one man
18 strangled him to death in the ensuing scuffle (don't
you idolize the diction of the powerful: *subdue* and
scuffle my oh my) and that the murder
that the killing of Arthur Miller on a Brooklyn
street was just a "justifiable accident" again
(again)

People been having accidents all over the globe
so long like that I reckon that the only
suitable insurance is a gun
I'm saying war is not to understand or rerun
war is to be fought and won

sometimes the feeling like amaze me baby
blots it out/the bestial but
not too often

tell me something
what you think would happen if
everytime they kill a black boy
then we kill a cop
everytime they kill a black man
then we kill a cop

you think the accident rate would lower
subsequently?

Sketching in the Transcendental

Through the long night the long trucks running the road

The wind in the white pines does not ululate like
that

Nor do the boreal meadowlands the mesopotamia
of the spirit does not sing

the song of the long trucks

The spirit differs
from a truck

a helluva lot

A Poem about Intelligence for My Brothers and Sisters

A few years back and they told me Black
means a hole where other folks
got brain/it was like the cells in the heads
of Black children was out to every hour on the hour naps
Scientists called the phenomenon the Notorious
Jensen Lapse, remember?
Anyway I was thinking
about how to devise
a test for the wise
like a Stanford-Binet
for the C.I.A.
you know?
Take Einstein
being the most the unquestionable the outstanding
the maximal mind of the century
right?
And I'm struggling against this lapse leftover
from my Black childhood to fathom why
anybody should say so:
$E = mc$ squared?
I try that on this old lady live on my block:
She sweeping away Saturday night from the stoop
and mad as can be because some absolute
jackass have left a kingsize mattress where
she have to sweep around it stains and all she
don't want to know nothing about in the first place
"Mrs. Johnson!" I say, leaning on the gate
between us: "What you think about somebody come up
with an E equals M C 2?"

"How you doin," she answer me, sideways, like she don't
want to let on she know I ain
combed my hair yet and here it is
Sunday morning but still I have the nerve
to be bothering serious work with these crazy
questions about
"*E* equals what you say again, dear?"
Then I tell her, "Well
also this same guy? I think
he was undisputed Father of the Atom Bomb!"
"That right." She mumbles or grumbles, not too politely
"And dint remember to wear socks when he put on
his shoes!" I add on (getting desperate)
at which point Mrs. Johnson take herself and her broom
a very big step down the stoop away from me
"And never did nothing for nobody in particular
lessen it was a committee
and
used to say, 'What time is it?'
and
you'd say, 'Six o'clock.'
and
he'd say, 'Day or night?'
and
and he never made nobody a cup a tea
in his whole brilliant life!"
"and
(my voice rises slightly)
and
he dint never boogie neither: never!"

"Well," say Mrs. Johnson, "Well, honey,
I do guess
that's genius for you."

verse from a fragmentary marriage

midtown manhattan
honk
beep
piss
shit
buzzbuzz
buzzbuzz
you
all over my mind and eyes

lilacs in starlight

midnight manhattan
you

all over
all over

for a while

1977: Poem for Mrs. Fannie Lou Hamer

You used to say, "June?
Honey when you come down here you
supposed to stay with me. Where
else?"
Meanin home
against the beer the shotguns and the
point of view of whitemen don'
never see Black anybodies without
some violent itch start up.
                          The ones who
said, "No Nigga's Votin in This Town . . .
lessen it be feet first to the booth"
Then jailed you
beat you brutal
bloody/battered/beat
you blue beyond the feeling
of the terrible

And failed to stop you.
Only God could but He
wouldn't stop
you
fortress from self-
pity

Humble as a woman anywhere
I remember finding you inside the laundromat
in Ruleville
          lion spine relaxed/hell
          what's the point to courage
          when you washin clothes?

But that took courage

>   just to sit there/target
>   to the killers lookin
>   for your singin face
>   perspirey through the rinse
>   and spin

and later
you stood mighty in the door on James Street
loud callin:

>   "BULLETS OR NO BULLETS!
>   THE FOOD IS COOKED
>   AN' GETTIN COLD!"

We ate
A family tremulous but fortified
by turnips/okra/handpicked
like the lilies

filled to the very living
full

one solid gospel
>   (*sanctified*)
one gospel
>   (*peace*)

one full Black lily
luminescent
in a homemade field

of love

Poem for South African Women

Commemoration of the 40,000 women and children who,
August 9, 1956, presented themselves in bodily protest against
the "dompass" in the capital of apartheid. Presented at The
United Nations, August 9, 1978.

Our own shadows disappear as the feet of thousands
by the tens of thousands pound the fallow land
into new dust that
rising like a marvelous pollen will be
fertile
even as the first woman whispering
imagination to the trees around her made
for righteous fruit
from such deliberate defense of life
as no other still
will claim inferior to any other safety
in the world

The whispers too they
intimate to the inmost ear of every spirit
now aroused they
carousing in ferocious affirmation
of all peaceable and loving amplitude
sound a certainly unbounded heat
from a baptismal smoke where yes
there will be fire

And the babies cease alarm as mothers
raising arms
and heart high as the stars so far unseen
nevertheless hurl into the universe
a moving force
irreversible as light years
traveling to the open
eye

And who will join this standing up
and the ones who stood without sweet company
will sing and sing
back into the mountains and
if necessary
even under the sea

we are the ones we have been waiting for

Notes on the Peanut

For the Poet David Henderson

Hi there. My name is George
Washington
Carver.
If you will bear with me
for a few minutes I
will share with you
a few
of the 30,117 uses to which
the lowly peanut has been put
by me
since yesterday afternoon.
If you will look at my feet you will notice
my sensible shoelaces made from unadulterated
peanut leaf composition that is biodegradable
in the extreme.
To your left you can observe the lovely Renoir
masterpiece reproduction that I have cleverly
pieced together from several million peanut
shell chips painted painstakingly so as to
accurately represent the colors of the original!
Overhead you will spot a squadron of Peanut B–52
Bombers flying due west.
I would extend my hands to greet you
at this time
except for the fact that I am holding a reserve
supply of high energy dry roasted peanuts
guaranteed to accelerate protein assimilation
precisely documented by my pocket peanut calculator;

May I ask when did you last contemplate the relationship
between the expanding peanut products' industry
and the development of post-Marxian economic theory
which (Let me emphasize) need not exclude moral attrition
of prepuberty
polymorphic
prehensible skills within the population age sectors
of 8 to 15?
I hope you will excuse me if I appear to be staring at you
through these functional yet high fashion and prescriptive
peanut contact lenses providing for the most
minute observation of your physical response to all of this
ultimately nutritional information.
Peanut butter peanut soap peanut margarine peanut
brick houses and house and field peanuts *per se* well
illustrate the diversified
potential of this lowly leguminous plant
to which you may correctly refer
also
as the goober the pindar the groundnut
and ground pea/let me
interrupt to take your name down on my
pocket peanut writing pad complete with matching
peanut pencil that only 3 or 4
chewing motions of the jaws will sharpen
into pyrotechnical utility
and no sweat.
Please:
Speak right into the peanut!

Your name?

Unemployment Monologue

You can call me Herbie Jr. or Ashamah
Kazaam. It don' matter much. The thing
is you don' wan' my name you
wanna mug shot
young
Black
male
who scares you chickenshit just
standin on the street just lookin
at you pass me by.
But I ain doin nothing I ain goin nowhere an
you
know it an
if you call me "Herbie" I don' mind
or "Junior"/that's all right
or "Ashamah Kazaam"/that's cool.
I say it don' really matter much
and then again/see
I may call you sweetmeat

I may call you tightass I might
one night I might break the windows
of the house you live in/I
might get tight and take your
wallet outasight/I might
hide out in the park to chase
you in the dark/etcetera/it
don' matter/I
may stay in school or quit
and I say
it
don' matter much
`you wanna mug shot
and the way I feel about it/well
so what?

you got it!

Toward a City that Sings

Into the topaz the crystalline signals
of Manhattan
the nightplane lowers my body
scintillate with longing to lie positive
beside
the electric waters of your flesh
and
I will never tell you the meaning of this poem:
Just say, "She wrote it and I recognize
the reference." Please
let it go at that. Although
it is all the willingness you lend
the world
as when you picked it up
the garbage scattering the cool
formalities of Madison Avenue
after midnight (where we walked
for miles as though we knew the woods
well enough to ignore the darkness)
although it is all the willingness you lend
the world
that makes me want
to clean up everything
in sight
(myself included)

for your possible
discovery

A Song of Sojourner Truth

Dedicated to Bernice Reagon

The trolley cars was rollin and the passengers all white
when Sojourner just decided it was time to take a seat
The trolley cars was rollin and the passengers all white
When Sojourner decided it was time to take a seat
It was time she felt to rest a while and ease up
on her feet
So Sojourner put her hand out
tried to flag the trolley down
So Sojourner put her hand out
for the trolley crossin town
And the driver did not see her
the conductor would not stop
But Sojourner yelled, "It's me!"
And put her body on the track
"It's me!" she yelled, "And yes,
I walked here but I ain walkin back!"
The trolley car conductor and the driver was afraid
to roll right over her and leave her lying dead
So they opened up the car and Sojourner took a seat
So Sojourner sat to rest a while and eased up on her feet

REFRAIN:

Sojourner had to be just crazy
tellin all that kinda truth
I say she musta been plain crazy
plus they say she was uncouth
talkin loud to any crowd
talkin bad insteada sad
She just had to be plain crazy
talkin all that kinda truth

If she had somewhere to go she said
I'll ride
If she had somewhere to go she said
I'll ride
jim crow or no
she said *I'll go*
just like the lady
that she was in all the knowing darkness
of her pride
she said *I'll ride*
she said *I'll talk*
she said *A Righteous Mouth*
ain nothin you should hide
she said she'd ride
just like the lady
that she was in all the knowing darkness
of her pride
she said *I'll ride*

They said she's Black and ugly and they said she's
really rough
They said if you treat her like a dog
well that'll be plenty good enough
And Sojourner said
I'll ride
And Sojourner said
I'll go
I'm a woman and this hell has made me tough
(Thank God!)
This hell has made me tough
I'm a strong Black woman
and Thank God!

REFRAIN:

Sojourner had to be just crazy
tellin all that kinda truth
I say she musta been plain crazy
plus they say she was uncouth
talkin loud to any crowd
talkin bad insteada sad
She just had to be plain crazy
talkin all that kinda truth

Alla Tha's All Right, but

Somebody come and carry me into a seven-day kiss
I can' use no historic no national no family bliss
I need an absolutely one to one a seven-day kiss

I can read the daily papers
I can even make a speech
But the news is stuff that tapers
down to salt poured in the breach

I been scheming about my people I been scheming about sex
I been dreaming about Africa and nightmaring Oedipus the Rex
But what I need is quite specific
terrifying rough stuff and terrific

I need an absolutely one to one a seven-day kiss
I can' use no more historic no national no bona fide family bliss
Somebody come and carry me into a seven-day kiss
Somebody come on
Somebody come on and carry me
over there!

Nightletters

You said, "In Morocco they make
                deliberate mistakes."

Next to you I do nothing
to perfect my safety

How should I dispel
the soul of such agile excitation?

Let no violence despoil
the sweet
translucent reasons for
our meeting

Once again I am wrong
but honestly

You walk away
and I am left to a maundering
through liberties

Already this wild beat leads me
to a stillness
opening

We are dangerous and undeniable/incense
in the English ivy
leaves

Evidently Looking at the Moon Requires a Clean Place to Stand

The forest dwindling narrow and irregular
to darken out the starlight on the ground
where needle shadows
signify the moon a harsh
a horizontal blink that lays the land
implicit to the movement of your body
is
the moon

You'd think I was lying to you
if I described precisely
how
implicit to the feeling of your lips
are luminous announcements
of more mystery than Arizona
more than just the imperturbable
convictions
of the cow

headfirst into a philosophy
and

so sexy
chewing up the grass

Free Flight

Nothing fills me up at night
I fall asleep for one or two hours then
up again my gut
alarms
I must arise
and wandering into the refrigerator
think about evaporated milk homemade vanilla ice cream
cherry pie hot from the oven with Something Like Vermont
Cheddar Cheese disintegrating luscious
on the top while
mildly
I devour almonds and raisins mixed to mathematical
criteria or celery or my very own sweet and sour snack
composed of brie peanut butter honey and
a minuscule slice of party size salami
on a single whole wheat cracker *no salt added*
or I read Cesar Vallejo/Gabriela Mistral/last year's
complete anthology or
I might begin another list of things to do
that starts with toilet paper and
I notice that I never jot down fresh
strawberry shortcake: never
even though fresh strawberry shortcake shoots down
raisins and almonds 6 to nothing
effortlessly
effortlessly
is this poem on my list?
light bulbs lemons envelopes ballpoint refill
post office and zucchini
oranges no
it's not
I guess that means I just forgot

walking my dog around the block leads
to a space in my mind where
during the newspaper strike questions
sizzle through suddenly like
Is there an earthquake down in Ecuador?
Did a TWA supersaver flight to San Francisco
land in Philadelphia instead
or
whatever happened to human rights
in Washington D.C.? Or what about downward destabilization
of the consumer price index
and I was in this school P.S. Tum-Ta-Tum and time came
for me to leave but
No! I couldn't leave: The Rule was anybody leaving
the premises without having taught somebody something
valuable would be henceforth proscribed from the
premises would be forever null and void/dull and
vilified well
I had stood in front of 40 to 50 students running my
mouth and I had been generous with deceitful smiles/soft-
spoken and pseudo-gentle wiles if and when forced
into discourse amongst such adults as constitutes
the regular treacheries of On The Job Behavior
ON THE JOB BEHAVIOR
is this poem on that list
polish shoes file nails coordinate tops and bottoms
lipstick control no
screaming I'm bored because
this is whoring away the hours of god's creation
pay attention to your eyes your hands the twilight
sky in the institutional big windows
no
I did not presume I was not so bold as to put this
poem on that list

then at the end of the class this boy gives me Mahler's 9th
symphony the double album listen
to it let it seep into you he
says transcendental love
he says
I think naw
I been angry all day long/nobody did the assignment
I am not prepared
I am not prepared for so much grace
the catapulting music of surprise that makes me
hideaway my face
nothing fills me up at night
yesterday the houseguest left a brown
towel in the bathroom for tonight
I set out a blue one and
an off-white washcloth seriously
I don't need no houseguest
I don't need no towels/lovers
I just need a dog

Maybe I'm kidding

Maybe I need a woman
a woman be so well you know so wifelike
so more or less motherly so listening so much
the universal skin you love to touch and who the
closer she gets to you the better she looks to me/somebody
say yes and make me laugh and tell me she know she
been there she spit bullets at my enemies she say you
need to sail around Alaska fuck it all try this new
cerebral tea and take a long bath

Maybe I need a man
a man be so well you know so manly so lifelike
so more or less virile so sure so much the deep
voice of opinion and the shoulders like a window
seat and cheeks so closely shaven by a twin-edged
razor blade no oily hair and no dandruff besides/
somebody say yes and make
me laugh and tell me he know he been there he spit
bullets at my enemies he say you need to sail around
Alaska fuck it all and take a long bath

lah-ti-dah and lah-ti-dum
what's this socialized obsession with the bathtub

Maybe I just need to love myself myself
(anyhow I'm more familiar with the subject)
Maybe when my cousin tells me you remind me
of a woman past her prime maybe I need
to hustle my cousin into a hammerlock
position make her cry out uncle and
I'm sorry
Maybe when I feel this horrible
inclination to kiss folks I despise
because the party's like that
an occasion to be kissing people
you despise maybe I should tell them kindly
kiss my

Maybe when I wake up in the middle of the night
I should go downstairs
dump the refrigerator contents on the floor
and stand there in the middle of the spilled milk
and the wasted butter spread beneath my dirty feet
writing poems
writing poems
maybe I just need to love myself myself and
anyway
I'm working on it

Letter to My Friend the Poet Ntozake Shange

Just back from Minnesota/North Dakota
All my clothes into the laundry or
dry cleaners before I leave
again
for Oregon then California
and my agent calls to say your business
manager is sending me
a Christmas present
from you
by messenger
within the next two hours: will
I be home?

Jesus Christ (I think) getting nervous
about two hours housebound
under the circumstances
maybe
one of us
better slow down!

Legend of the Holy Night When the Police Finally Held Fire

For Gwendolen Hardwick

Small as a mustard seed
from the nile and nubile kingdom
where the young God secretly
created conga drums
from sapling trees and slender skin
then blew a breeze between
two new
tumescent
beech leaves
for the full lips
playing of the flute

Transplanted to the rigid terrors
firm like trigger to the gun
she runs
she runs for life
confronts the cops
she stops
she cocks her large eyes
lock into courageous
accusation

Mothafuckas: Shoot me
Can't you see
me?
Shoot me: Mothafuckas
What?

Even they can see the mustard seed
the trembling river and the totem
trees

They do not shoot/inside the kingdom
where you
come from

A Poem About Vieques, Puerto Rico

In Vieques
"The Ocean Is Closed on Mondays"

Frank the Bartender is full of information:
"So this guy, a guest, here at the hotel,
says to me, there aren't any face cloths."

So I said to him, "Sit down."

He sat down. Then I said to him, "If
you were in Paradise
would you expect to find a face
cloth?"

If you were in Paradise
would you expect to find the U.S. Navy
and the Marines bombing the hell
out of the land/mining the waters
and throwing indigenous birds indigenous
trees into extinction?

Where sugarcane and pineapples
and locust trees and mango and
where soursop/acacia palm
and lusciously
gardenias/amaropa/bougainvillea
grew so beautiful
in Paradise would
you expect to find the river gulleys
dried down to the dustbone of the earth/
and all the grass turned into tinderstuff?

At the hotel
Frank the Bartender says: "Jamaica?
                         No. I never had the time!"

Helen and her husband Tom tell me:
"Isn't it interesting how
the Haitians are
compared to the other islander peoples
so incredibly artistic!
But do you know the story how that happened?
It was a Swede. A man named
—what was his name? *Olafson*
I'm sure: yes: Olafson.
He came, this Swede, to Haiti
and he saw the possibilities
for artistic expression among the natives
there. So he encouraged, he taught them
to do it
That's the story!"

In Vieques there are these words painted white
on the night road

Vieques Si
Navy NO

Navy FUERA
(NAVY OUT)

y

Rádame Fidel Castro

At the Hotel
Frank the Bartender says:

"So I'm with this girl down on the beach
one night
and I'm giving it to her
I'm going for broke
I'm working myself out
pumping away
up and down
up and down
and I say to her
Is it in?
And she says
NO
Put it in! I yell
So I'm going on like crazy
Is it in? I ask her again
Yeah, she says
Oh, for crissakes, I tell her:
In that case, put it back
put it back in the sand."

I am lying on the sand
trying to relax under the spectacular sky
the Hollywood clouds looking quite superlative
in blue
y
los hombres me llaman así:
Hey, honey
Hey, darling
ssswssssw ssswsssw!
(Entonces)
Hey, Black Gurrl!

Last night a horse followed me home
I kept feeling there was something behind me
And there was:
A horse

His ribs glittering silver
under the tight soft colored skin
of his body, and there
wasn't any drinkable water in sight
or sound
and I noticed the hills around us dry
to the point where even Ingmar Bergman
couldn't eke out sensuality
from that ground
from the figure of that animal
standing hungry on that ground
no sensuallty

and you may get the idea that the United States'
military establishment is Humphrey Bogart
cracking up all over the screen or Henry
Fonda sorry or Burt Lancaster screwing
whatshername
in the klieglit surf

but last night
this horse followed me home
in Vieques
in Paradise

and he was starved out

and as a matter of fact
this movie: the horse and the children and the flowers and
the fish and the coconuts and
the sea itself in Vieques

Jesus Christ!
Put it back!
Put it back!
In the sand!

The point of this movie
is
a pretty rough fuck.

Inaugural Rose

Wanting to stomp down Eighth Avenue snow
or no snow where you might be so we
can takeover the evening by taxi
by kerosene lamp by literal cups of tea

that you love me

wanting to say, "Jesus, I'm glad. And I am not
calm: Not calm!" But I
am shy. And shy is short
on reach and wide on bowing
out. It's in:
against the flint and deep
irradiation of this torso listing
to the phosphorescence of French windows in
the bells/your hair/the forehead
of the morning of your face a clear
a calm decision of the light
to gather there

And you an obstinate an elegant
nail-bitten hand on quandaries of self-correction/
self-perfection as political as building your own
bed to tell the truth in
And your waist as narrow as the questions
you insist upon palpate/

expose immense not knowing any of the words
to say *okay* or *wrong*

And my wanting to say
wanting to show and tell *bells/*
okay because I'm shy
but I
will not lie

to you

En Passant

A white man tells me he told a white woman

You need to be fucked to death
You need a Black man

She said: What would my family say?

I say the same thing: What would my family
say
about that?

For Li'l Bit

Pointing to the middle of your forehead where a white
stripe (you say) marks the face of a demonic
destiny that you (a Black woman without
any visible marking of the soft skin easily
exact easily covering the definite
image of the ambiguous skull) insist on knowing in advance
or after the fact of perhaps divinity perhaps a character
curse revealed by power or by pain astonishing
an afternoon/you emphasize the problem of
the stripe the white disfigurement above your
eyes: you finger the place of such thin
skin where the real scar shows itself through its
invisibility: I look but I can only see a swollen
vein of painful declaration leading to the clarity
the cradle songs crude histories invent

"My mother took this picture of me as a little girl.
You could see it. Right here it was: A white
stripe. And I held the picture in
my hands. I held the picture of me
in my hands. But now it's lost.
I don't know what happened.
To the photograph. But look. You can
still see the stripe: The mark."

You point to the middle of your forehead where a white
stripe (you say) marks the face of a stranger a problematic
destiny and I watch the trembling of your index finger

my own heart shaken as I watch you (only one
Black woman kneeling on the floor) attempt to trace
to feel (in small) the meaning of the forced
the barbarous amalgamation that enchains
you with such pain: my sister blamed by names
and blamed by body into far configurations love
cannot entirely control:

Stand up to sweat away the wound
Stand up to dance away the snow
Or
let me kneel
beside you

Niagara Falls

Dedicated to Leonard Bernstein

And in the first place the flowing of the river
went about its business like a hulking
shallows curling ankle deep to spume

and in the second place the flowing river
fell
and falling fell stupendous
down
a breakneck cliff invisible behind
the cataclysmic streaming burst apart
at bottom
into spray that birds
attempted to delay by calmly
playing in the serpentine formations
of the frothing aftermath

and then in my place stood a fool
surprised by power that wins only
peace as when the sliding clouds collide
into a new perfection

quietly

calling it quits

honey dripping rain through the spruce
tree blossoms sticky in the sun
after the storm
aftermath to hatred dissolute in bed
the storm
the teasing up of deepsea animals flung
to a brawling surface
skewered wild by wind and moonstone
torturing
the tides into a finicky
fulfillment

a mirage

now wanes the moon the ocean
slides away
my love collects
itself

apart from you

Poem toward the Bottom Line

Then this is the truth: That we began here
where no road existed even
as a dream: where staggered scream and grief inside
the howling air where hunched against
the feeling and the sounds of beast we moved
the left and then the right leg: stilted terminals
against infinity against amorphous omnivores
against the frozen vertigo of all
position: there we moved against
the hungering for heat for ease we moved
as now we move against each
other unpredictable around the corner
of this sweet occasion. Or as now the earth
assumes the skeletal that just the snow that just
the body of your trusting me can capture

tenderly enough.

Memoranda toward the Spring of Seventy-Nine

The Shah of Iran was overthrown
by only several million mostly un-
armed/inside agitators.

■

The Daily News reports that one American
among the first to be evacuated, Patsy
Farness of Seattle, said she somehow en-
joyed the whole thing. Coming off the plane
with two Persian cats and a poodle, she said:
"It was a lovely experience. I didn't want
to leave."

■

The instruction booklet for cooking with a
Chinese wok declares as follows: "With use
your wok will acquire the blackened look of
distinction."

■

Martin Luther King, Jr., is still dead.
The sponsor for the memorial program on
his birthday is The National Boat Show
at the Coliseum running January 13th through
the 21st and open to the public.

■

If only I could stay awake until 3
then
on Channel Eleven
I could watch Part One of Adolf Hitler
but
then I'd be too tired to get up by 8
to watch Kaptain Kangaroo and Woody Woodpecker
on Channels 2 and 5.

■

The Shah of Iran was overthrown
by only several million mostly un-
armed/inside agitators.

■

There must be something else on television.

■

Martin Luther King, Jr., is still dead.

■

Dear Abby,

The idea is two dozen red roses
but
there isn't any form around the house.
Please advise.

A Short Note to My Very Critical and Well-Beloved Friends and Comrades

First they said I was too light
Then they said I was too dark
Then they said I was too different
Then they said I was too much the same
Then they said I was too young
Then they said I was too old
Then they said I was too interracial
Then they said I was too much a nationalist
Then they said I was too silly
Then they said I was too angry
Then they said I was too idealistic
Then they said I was too confusing altogether:
Make up your mind! They said. Are you militant
or sweet? Are you vegetarian or meat? Are you straight
or are you gay?

And I said, Hey! It's not about *my* mind.

Rape Is Not a Poem

1

One day she saw them coming into the garden
where the flowers live.
They
found the colors beautiful and
they discovered the sweet smell
that the flowers held
so
they stamped upon and tore apart
the garden
just because (they said)
those flowers?
They were asking for it.

2

I let him into the house to say hello.
"Hello," he said.
"Hello," I said.
"How're you?" he asked me.
"Not bad," I told him.
"You look great," he smiled.
"Thanks; I've been busy: I am busy."
"Well, I guess I'll be heading out, again,"
he said.
"Okay," I answered and, "Take care," I said.
"I'm gonna do just that," he said.
"No!" I said: "No! Please don't. Please
leave me alone. Now. No. Please!" I said.

"I'm leaving," he laughed: "I'm leaving you
alone; I'm going now!"
"No!" I cried: "No. Please don't do this to me!"
But he was not talking anymore and there was
nothing else that I could say
to make him listen
to me.

3

And considering your contempt
And considering my hatred consequent to that
And considering the history
that leads us to this dismal place where (your arm
raised
and my eyes
lowered)
there is nothing left but the drippings
of power and
a consummate wreck of tenderness/I
want to know:
Is this what you call
Only Natural?

4

My dog will never learn the names
of stars or thorns but
fully he
encounters whatever it is
shits on the ground
then finds a fallen leaf still holding
raindrops from the day and
there he stays

a big dog
(licking at the tiny water)
delicate as he is
elsewhere
fierce

You should let him teach you how
to come down

Memo:

When I hear some woman say she
has finally decided you can spend time with
other women, I wonder what she means: Her
mother? My mother?
I've always despised my woman friends. Even
if they introduced me to a man I found
attractive I have never let them become
what you could call my intimates. Why
should I? Men are the ones with the money and
the big way with waiters and the passkey
to excitement in strange places of real
danger and the power to make things happen
like babies or war and all these great ideas
about mass magazines for members of the weaker sex
who need permission
to eat potatoes or a doctor's opinion on orgasm after death
or the latest word on what the female
executive should do, after hours, wearing
what. They must be morons: women!
Don't you think?
I guess you could say
I'm stuck in my ways
as
That Cosmopolitan Girl.

What Is This in Reference To?
or
We Must Get Together Sometime Soon!

Hello.
I'm sorry.
I can't talk to you.
I am unavailable.
I am out of the house.
I am out of town.
I am out of the country.
I am out of my mind.
I am indisposed.
The cat has my tongue.
Please do not hang up.
I know this is frustrating
                    ridiculous
                    solipsistic
                    inconvenient
                    mechanical
                    and
                    a pain in the ass
Please listen for the beep.
When you hear the beep
please leave a message as long as you like
or better still

please leave a brief message
or better yet
state your purpose in concise
readily decipherable terms and be sure
to leave your name your number
the time
the date
the place
and a list of the secret desires underlying this conventional
even hackneyed outreach represented
by
your call.
This is your dime.
Listen for the beep. Sucker.

Poem #2 for Inaugural Rose

Calling you from my kitchen to the one where you cook
for strangers and it hits me how we fall
into usefulness/change into steak or sausage or
(more frequently) fried chicken
like glut to the gluttonous/choosing a leg a poem
a voice and even a smile a breast/dark or light moments
of the mind: how
they throw out the rest or adjudicate the best of our
feeling/inedible because somersault singing in silence
will not flake to the fork at 425 or any kind of cue
will not do
and joy is not nice on ice: joy is not nice
But thinking about you over there at the stove
while I sit near the sink and we are not turkey/
I am not ham or bananas/nothing about you
reminds me of money or grist for the fist
and so on and so on but outside you know there is
rain to no purpose in the cockroach concrete of this
common predicament
and I find myself transfixed by the downpour un-
necessarily beating my blood up to the (something inside me
wants to say the *visual instinct of your face* or
sometimes I need to write Drums to Overcome the Terrors
of Iran but really
it's about the) grace the chimerical
rising of your own and secret eyes to surprise
and to surprise
and to surprise

me

Poem about My Rights

Even tonight and I need to take a walk and clear
my head about this poem about why I can't
go out without changing my clothes my shoes
my body posture my gender identity my age
my status as a woman alone in the evening/
alone on the streets/alone not being the point/
the point being that I can't do what I want
to do with my own body because I am the wrong
sex the wrong age the wrong skin and
suppose it was not here in the city but down on the beach/
or far into the woods and I wanted to go
there by myself thinking about God/or thinking
about children or thinking about the world/all of it
disclosed by the stars and the silence:
I could not go and I could not think and I could not
stay there
alone
as I need to be
alone because I can't do what I want to do with my own
body and
who in the hell set things up
like this
and in France they say if the guy penetrates
but does not ejaculate then he did not rape me

and if after stabbing him if after screams if
after begging the bastard and if even after smashing
a hammer to his head if even after that if he
and his buddies fuck me after that
then I consented and there was
no rape because finally you understand, finally
they fucked me over because I was wrong, I was
wrong again to be me being me where I was/wrong
to be who I am
which is exactly like South Africa
penetrating into Namibia penetrating into
Angola and does that mean I mean how do you know if
Pretoria ejaculates what will the evidence look like the
proof of the monster jackboot ejaculation on Blackland
and if
after Namibia and if after Angola and if after Zimbabwe
and if after all of my kinsmen and women resist even to
self-immolation of the villages and if after that
we lose nevertheless what will the big boys say will they
claim my consent:
Do You Follow Me: We are the wrong people of
the wrong skin on the wrong continent and what
in the hell is everybody being reasonable about
and according to the *Times* this week
back in 1966 the C.I.A. decided that they had this problem
and the problem was a man named Nkrumah so they
killed him and before that it was Patrice Lumumba
and before that it was my father on the campus
of my Ivy League school and my father afraid
to walk into the cafeteria because he said he
was wrong the wrong age the wrong skin the wrong
gender identity and he was paying my tuition and

before that
it was my father saying I was wrong saying that
I should have been a boy because he wanted one/a
boy and that I should have been lighter skinned and
that I should have had straighter hair and that
I should not be so boy crazy but instead I should
just be one/a boy and before that
it was my mother pleading plastic surgery for
my nose and braces for my teeth and telling me
to let the books loose to let them loose in other
words
I am very familiar with the problems of the C.I.A.
and the problems of South Africa and the problems
of Exxon Corporation and the problems of white
America in general and the problems of the teachers
and the preachers and the F.B.I. and the social
workers and my particular Mom and Dad/I am very
familiar with the problems because the problems
turn out to be
me
I am the history of rape
I am the history of the rejection of who I am
I am the history of the terrorized incarceration of
my self
I am the history of battery assault and limitless
armies against whatever I want to do with my mind
and my body and my soul and
whether it's about walking out at night
or whether it's about the love that I feel or
whether it's about the sanctity of my vagina or
the sanctity of my national boundaries
or the sanctity of my leaders or the sanctity
of each and every desire

that I know from my personal and idiosyncratic
and indisputably single and singular heart
I have been raped
be-
cause I have been wrong the wrong sex the wrong age
the wrong skin the wrong nose the wrong hair the
wrong need the wrong dream the wrong geographic
the wrong sartorial I
I have been the meaning of rape
I have been the problem everyone seeks to
eliminate by forced
penetration with or without the evidence of slime and/
but let this be unmistakable this poem
is not consent I do not consent
to my mother to my father to the teachers to
the F.B.I. to South Africa to Bedford-Stuy
to Park Avenue to American Airlines to the hardon
idlers on the corners to the sneaky creeps in
cars
I am not wrong: Wrong is not my name
My name is my own my own my own
and I can't tell you who the hell set things up like this
but I can tell you that from now on my resistance
my simple and daily and nightly self-determination
may very well cost you your life

Grand Army Plaza

For Ethelbert

Why would anybody build a monument to civil war?

The tall man and myself tonight
we will not sleep together
we may not
either one of us
sleep
in any case
the differential between friend and lover
is a problem
definitions curse
as *nowadays we're friends*
or
we were lovers once
while
overarching the fastidious the starlit
dust
that softens space between us
is the history that bleeds
through shirt and blouse
alike

the stain of skin on stone

But on this hard ground curved by memories
of union and disunion and of brothers dead
by the familiar hand

how do we face to face a man
a woman
interpenetrated
free
and reaching still toward the kiss that will
not suffocate?

We are not survivors of a civil war

We survive our love
because we go on

loving

Taking Care

Dedicated to the Poet Sekou Sundiata and to the Students of
SUNY at Stony Brook

1

Down on East Pratt Street in Baltimore
where the bar on the corner and the frozen foods
grocery store look alike: (They're both closed
on weekdays or open only to rats too lazy to keep up
with the newstuff in town)
even the couple the police separated when one
night either she was going to scream his head off or
he meant to knock her teeth down her throat
(because the regular the identical
conjugal argument of their evenings together
about a flirtation or a misinterpretation from eleven
years ago in a bar that was
unmistakably wide open when whatever went down that
they couldn't seem to forget about
except at the certain risk of boredom worse
than violent horseplay enough to wake the neighbors from
related habits of monogamous monotony) even that separated
couple stays married
where
two guys measure each other
to a grim finesse: one wants to continue
slashing the skin from the young tree the city
planted outside the small
brick house of the other and the guy with the knife
and the anger and the tree and the guy
with the expectation of a bigger and a bigger and
a bigger tree outside his narrow
brick house apparently feel mixed about whether
the disagreement of the moment merits attempted
or accomplished homicide

in Baltimore the point about the stone steps
the white stonestairs that women wash
as frequently as underwear
the point is what else
should you try
to take care of
East Pratt Street is not Whopping Hollow Road
and whopping hollow is not Telegraph Avenue
not telepathy
among the birds
and Baltimore not Bali Hai
although they sell a lot of that
in bottles
the city squats as sized down as regulated
as predictable as elementary
school classroom
buildings mostly
sacrilegious/sacramental
Baltimore   Baltimore

2

The boss man tell you: "For the little woman
                              nothing is too much:

                              Promise her anything
                              but give her
                              Rhodesia"

3

I see people leaving Stony Brook
bound for Portland Oregon
Humboldt's current
God's will
ridiculous redwood memories
free coastline/any exponential
wilderness to yell out
loud I love where rising
tides flood land to action
uninhibited
harmonious
and singular

4

Even if the trail turns back to Baltimore
I figure we (become familiar
with mashed fingers
flatfeet and the deadpan and
become acquainted with the dervish possibilities
of freak and roll and glide inside
no space)

I figure we (amazing transmutations/heavyweight
deposits of the soul)
can body forth this ship together
keep it in the water
balancing
or take it out
as far as we can go
drydock

but deep

A Right-to-Lifer in Grand Forks, North Dakota

For Sandy Donaldson

We stayed.
Through finger drifts and drifts to bury trees.
Men frozen on the road home from town.
Babies dead because the doctor could not see
the house for the snow.
Women dead from death.
Children trained to trust the first door the nearest
hand.
River flood.
Mud.
Wind down from Canada.
Blizzards from hell.
Winter long as life.
We stayed.
After the Buffalo.
After the Indians.
After the westward hustling types.
After the sunrise.
We stayed.
On land big and empty as the entire sky.
We stayed.
Sugar beets.
Barley.
Sunflowers.
Wheat.
Potatoes.
Sure:
We stayed.
Right to life?
Hell, yeah!
What you suppose this trouble's been
all about?

From America: A Poem in Process

Dedicated to Christopher David Meyer

St. Paul, Minnesota

Ice
Between me and the earth itself it's ice
between me and the single runners single
houses single cars slid wide on ice
it's ice
between me and the breath I need to melt
the frozen mouth of something soft
something mud
something conversational perhaps
it's ice

I walk across the roots of trees
enormous elm tree shelters from the faraway
firing stars
elm trees scribbling a confusion of dark branches
that must mystify the simple
sky stretched into cloudy scar
tissues torn by snow and sleet interruptions
of a wan and waning
moan

I hear no whispering no shout no scream

I walk particular to keep upright the whole head cold
stung tight: It's pick and toe to cross the ice
the massive avenues a fascist scale a
monumental holding action under gossamer
and glossy hoar frost assault

sweet home
sweet home
oh lord:I wonder
if I'm ever gone get
home

Carrying paperbag provisions from a supermarket
and the wolves leap closer howling
from the corners of a formal place
where little moves besides the moon
I am too small
to change anything at all
I am too small
to change anything at all
where little moves besides the moon

Grand Forks, North Dakota

Around March and the crows
come back
flying low over the bodies when
the drifts melt down
flying low
looking for the eyes
where eight miles straight ahead
or seven miles behind
it's just the same in January
side to side
the same.
It's white.
It's flat.
(If you stood on top a beer can you could probably see
Mexico.)

One year a country wife went crazy from the winter
all that white around her up above
and underfoot the white was everywhere
too much: She hid away inside her mud
home on the prairie
and her husband just to please
her one day painted up the mud walls white
That lady killed herself

And in the beginning
was the buffalo

(How long does an epiphany take?)

The Red River and The Red Lake River
become the Red River North flowing North
The land becomes the reason why the world
is flat but infinite
Ice becomes the snow becomes the snirt (the topsoil blown
berserk but softly blown)
Sky becomes much more than left or right eyes can pretend
to comprehend even
incorrectly
Cars become the trunk filled with emergency supplies of candles
granola bars and plastic garbage bags against the oneway wind
Time becomes two minutes to pneumonia two minutes to the death
of flesh in 45 degrees below
The face becomes remote from comedy and open to whatever heats
the heart
The mind becomes a cantilever: fair is
fair: "There's peace and quiet in
Grand Forks," he told me: "There's the
Air Force and the missile bases too: Fair
is fair," he
shrugs.

Lexington, Kentucky

I wish I was a horse
had me a groom
a stable boy a jockey
and a master starve himself
to buy me hay
I wish I was a horse
had me plantations full of grass
for grazing and a swimming pool
and one helluva pretty city
upside down to watch me race
some other horse
every now and then

I wish I was a horse
couldn't read about nothing
couldn't read about some local boy
the daily papers
said they asked him what kind of school he'd
like
the boy said he'd "rather just
be hit by a truck" what
kind of a fool boy is that
in Lexington Kentucky
there's a railroad crossing
holds down traffic to a lengthy idle
while
the coal cars trundle through
The Burlington Northern
coal cars weighting 200,000 pounds each
coal car carrying its weight again 200,000 pounds
of coal: I reckon takes good track to carry that
a heavy rail

I hear they throw on up to three of them high-
powered engines each one 450,000 pounds at 3/4 of a million
dollars each to pull 100 coal cars taking the goodies
out of Eastern Kentucky
where the only respite for the two-legged
variety of inhabitant is serious or fatal
injury
where
in relationship to The Red River North and The Red
Lake River flowing North
am I
too small
to change anything at all?

In Transit

Black children traveling north from Tuscaloosa
Alabama into Lexington sing *Sweet*
Home
Sweet Home
Oh Lord
I wonder if I'm ever
gone get home
where
in relationship to The Burlington Northern Railroad
is
that song?

My own child tells me: "You
walk past
any railroad siding
and you hear the engines: just purring away"